IN THE BEGINNING

tales from the Old Testament
retold for children

In the Beginning
© 2023 North Parade Publishing,
Written by Janice Emmerson
Illustrations by QBS Learning

Published by North Parade Publishing, Bath BA1 1LF, United Kingdom

All rights are reserved. No part of this publication may be reproduced, stored in a retrieval system or transmitted in any form or by any means, electronic, mechanical, photocopying, recording or otherwise, without the prior permission of the Publisher

Printed in China

Contents

In the Beginning — 4
Genesis 1–2

The Forbidden Fruit — 10
Genesis 3

The First Murder — 13
Genesis 4

Noah and the Big Boat — 14
Genesis 6–7

The Rain Comes — 17
Genesis 7–8

The Wonderful Promise — 21
Genesis 9

Sky High — 22
Genesis 11

Father of a Nation — 24
Genesis 12, 15

In the Beginning

In the beginning there was nothing. Nothing at all. No light, no dark. No land, no sea. No giraffes, no dolphins. No cars, no televisions. Nothing. Absolutely nothing.

Then God created the heavens and the earth. From nothing!

But still everything was covered in darkness. So God spoke. "Let there be light!" he said. And because God had said it, there was light.

God was pleased. He separated the light from the darkness, and so he made the first day and the first night, with morning and evening in between. And that was the very first day. Then God separated the water into two parts, and in between them he made the sky. That was the second day.

On the third day, God separated the water from the dry land, and he named the dry land "earth", and the water that was gathered together "seas". And from the earth grew many plants—soft green grass, rippling fields of corn, and tall, towering oak trees. And God was pleased.

On the fourth day, God chose to put wonderful lights in the sky—the fiery life-giving sun, the cool mysterious moon, and all the bright winking stars that shine when everything else is dark.

On the fifth day, God filled the waters with huge sea animals and little fishes and wobbly jellyfish, and in the sky he placed all sorts of birds, from colourful parrots and curious robins, to proud eagles and sleepy owls.

On the sixth day, God made animals of all shapes and sizes to slither and crawl and leap and run upon the earth. He made slinking snakes, and jumping frogs, lumbering elephants, and fleet-footed cheetahs.

Then God made something else, something very special. He made the very first people. He made them in his own image, to look like him. First he made a man, Adam, and then, to be his companion, he made the first woman, Eve. He showed them this wonderful world that he had made and told them to look after it.

And God was pleased with all he had done.

Everything was finished, just as God had planned. And so, on the seventh day, God took some time out. He made this a special day—a holy day. A day to stop and rest and think about things.

The Forbidden Fruit

In the midst of this wonderful world that he had created, God made an extra special place for Adam and Eve to live—a beautiful garden filled with fruit trees, so that they might never go hungry. God only gave them one rule—they were not to eat the fruit of the Tree of Knowledge that he had planted in the middle of the garden.

Now, the snake was the most cunning of all the animals that God had created. He told Eve that the fruit would make her wise like God, and persuaded her to eat some. Eve was tempted. She took a bite, and gave some to Adam, and he too ate from the forbidden tree.

In that instance everything changed. Adam and Eve felt different. Everything felt different. Apart from anything else, they both realised at exactly the same time that they were naked. They were wearing nothing at all! Five minutes ago that hadn't been a problem, but now they felt embarrassed and ashamed, and slunk away among the plants to hide.

When God called down to them, he found them still hiding and cowering in the shadows. "What have you done?" he said. But he knew. He knew what they had done, and he knew that nothing could be the same from now on.

In anger God cursed the snake to crawl on its belly for the rest of its life, and with a heart filled with disappointment, he told Adam and Eve that from now on they would have to work for their food. No longer would it just drop into their hands. They would have to work the land, and battle against weeds and thorns.

Then he sadly banished Adam and Eve from the beautiful garden, and sent them out into the world, clothed in animal skins that he made for them. At the entrance to the garden he placed an angel with a flaming sword to stand guard.

The First Murder

The years passed. Adam and Eve now had two sons—Cain, who was a farmer who worked in the fields, and Abel, a shepherd. One day, they brought offerings to God. Cain brought some of the food he had grown, while his brother brought the finest meat, from his best lamb. Abel wanted to offer God the very best he had.

When God accepted his brother's offering and not his, Cain was furious. He felt hurt and jealous and bitter, and in a fit of rage he knocked his brother to the ground and killed him.

God was sad and angry. He knew exactly what had happened, and he could see that Cain wasn't at all sorry for what he had done. He told Cain that he would never have a permanent home, and sent him away from his family to wander from place to place.

Noah and the Big Boat

More years passed. The land became filled with more and more people—and those people did bad things.

It broke God's heart. He had made such a beautiful world for humans, and they had become so wicked. He wished he had never made them. In fact, he decided to wash his world clean and start all over again.

But there was one man on earth who was good. One man who *did* love and obey God. His name was Noah, and he had three sons—Shem, Ham and Japheth.

God spoke to Noah. "I'm going to send a great flood," he told him. "I'm going to wash all the wicked people off the face of the earth. But I want you to build a big boat for yourself and your family. In fact, it will have to be very big, because I want you to gather two of every kind of creature on the earth, one male and one female. Every bird, every animal, everything that creeps or crawls. And you will have to leave enough room for plenty of food!"

This was a strange request. It wasn't even raining. And Noah was probably nowhere close to the sea. But Noah trusted in God. If God told him that this was what he must do, then this was what he would do.
It didn't matter if anyone else laughed at him, or made fun of him.
Noah was building a boat.

And build a boat he did. With the help of his sons and with a lot of hard work, the boat was finally finished.

When the boat was completed, God spoke again to Noah. He told him to gather together his family and all the animals, for in just seven days the rain was going to begin.

The Rain Comes

Sure enough, in seven days the clouds grew dark and heavy and the first raindrops fell. Maybe to begin with, people were quite pleased. Maybe they needed rain for their crops. But it kept raining. Now it wouldn't have been so pleasant, with the sky dark and ominous, and the ground turned to mud. On it rained. The rivers burst their banks, the water came up from underground springs, and everywhere you looked there was water. And on it rained. The rooftops weren't safe. People made for the hills. But still it rained. Now the hills were underwater and even the mountains weren't safe.

For forty days and forty nights it rained and it rained, and by the end, there was no land to be seen. Everywhere was covered in water. No fields, no hills, no towns, no cities. Just one big sea.

And one big boat. Well, actually, it looked rather small now, as it floated on the vast, endless ocean.

But Noah and all his family were safe, just as God had promised. For many months they lived onboard that gigantic boat. For another 150 days the whole world was covered in water. But at the end of that time, God sent a wind to blow over the earth, and slowly, slowly, the water began to recede.

At last the boat touched land—the top of a mountain range! After a while Noah sent out a raven, and then a dove, to see if they could find dry land. But the dove flew back, for it could find nowhere to land. A week later, he sent it out again. Again it flew back, but this time it held an olive leaf in its beak. How exciting that must have been!

After another week had passed, Noah sent the dove out yet again. And this time it didn't return! Noah knew that this meant the time had come for him and his family and all the animals to finally leave the boat and start a new life on God's spring-cleaned world.

The Wonderful Promise

God promised to never again send such a dreadful flood, and to show Noah that he meant what he said (which God always does) he placed a beautiful rainbow in the sky.

"Whenever I see this rainbow," God told Noah, "I'll remember the promise that I made to you and every living creature on this earth."

Sky High

Time passed. To begin with there was only one language on earth. There were many, many people now, for Noah's sons had had children of their own, and they had had children of *their* own, and so on, and so on … but everyone could understand everyone else because they all spoke the same language.

There came a time when some of Noah's descendents decided to settle down and build a permanent place to live. They planned to build a wonderful city, the crowning glory of which would be a magnificent tower, that reached up into the very clouds.

"Then everyone will come from miles around to see," they boasted to one another. "We'll be famous!"

And so work started on the tower, and brick by brick it began to rise out of the ground, higher and higher. And the people were very pleased with themselves.

God looked down upon the city and the tower. He was not happy. They were becoming proud and vain. They had forgotten about God!

"They think they can do anything because they all speak the same language," said God to himself. "We'll see about that!"

All at once the city was filled with noise—all the people were speaking in different languages. It sounded like gobbledygook! They were speaking in Ancient Greek and Latin and Arabic and Hebrew and who knew what else? (Well, God knew, obviously).

And work stopped—no one could understand anyone else, so it made it rather difficult to get anything done. After a while they all wandered off in different directions, and were scattered across the earth. Along with their languages.

And the tower became known as the Tower of Babel.

Father of a Nation

Abraham was a good man. Like Noah before him, he trusted in God with all of his heart. So when God told him to pack up his stuff, gather his wife Sarah, his nephew, and his servants, leave everything that he knew, and head to Canaan, well, that is exactly what he did. And in return for Abraham's trust and love and obedience, God promised to bless him.

One night, Abraham had a vision. God showed him the sky. "Look at all the stars," God said. "Your family will be like that. So many that you can't count! Because of your faith, every nation on earth will be blessed through your children, and your children's children!"

And it happened just as God promised—Abraham became the father of many nations, and from the line of his descendents came the Saviour of mankind, Jesus Christ the Redeemer.

The great story had truly begun!